Medication Explained

Essential English for Pharmacists

現場で役立つ薬学英語表現

Glenn D. Gagné

NAN'UN-DO

Medication Explained

Essential English for Pharmacists

Copyright © 2019

by Glenn D. Gagné

All Rights Reserved
No part of this book may be reproduced in any form
without written permission from the authors and Nan'un-do Co., Ltd.

PREFACE

Background:

Imagine being sick in a foreign country where you do not understand the language. To make matters worse, what if you weren't able to read the medicine explanation? This is the situation for many visitors and foreign residents in Japan. They cannot understand Japanese and cannot even look up the words in dictionaries because they are written in "Kanji," Chinese characters.

In such a situation, a pharmacist who can explain medicine in English is a great help. Even when English is not the native language of the foreign resident, it is much more widely understood than Japanese.

Objective:

This textbook presents a patient-centered approach to help Japanese pharmacists explain medicine in English.

Method:

The language introduced is intended for patients who are not in the medical profession. Thus, "everyday English" is recommended instead of medical terminology. For example, the terms "pain reliever" or "painkiller" are suggested, rather than "analgesic."

The textbook presents a four-part framework for explaining medicine quickly, clearly, and concisely.
   1) What the medicine is
   2) How to administer the medicine
   3) Precautions
   4) Storage methods

This framework allows both student and teacher to focus on specific points without losing focus on the overall objective of explaining medicine.

Material is introduced step by step, and many exercises are given to practice what has been learned. Learning tasks start out easy and become progressively more difficult, resulting in a series of mini-successes which motivate the students to move forward.

After learning the basics, role-play activities are then set up and practiced. By the end of the course, students will be able to put into active use what they have learned.

ACKNOWLEDGMENTS

I would like to thank the faculty, staff, and students of the School of Pharmacy of Aichi Gakuin University for their help and cooperation during the writing of this book.

I would like to thank the editorial staff at NAN'UN-DO, especially, my patient editor Hiromi Ito, and my proofeaders Michael Critchley, and Mitsuko Hirai.

I would also like to thank my many unofficial editors including: Hiroshi Usami, Richard Coutu (Pharm. D), Jennifer M. Gagné (PhD, Cell & Molecular Biology), Michael Coutu, Brendan Kelleher, David Pomatti, Jeff Blair, and Vick Ssali for their advice while making this textbook.

I would like to thank my wife for her support, helping with multiple drafts of the book and taking care of the boys.

Finally, I would like to thank my first and best teacher, my mom, for giving me my inspiration.

CONTENTS

PREFACE	3
UNIT 1 Introduction to Explaining Medicine	6
UNIT 2 Types of Medicine: "What is this?"	10
UNIT 3 Symptoms: "What is it for?"	14
UNIT 4 Learning Lab: Medicine Types and Purpose	20
UNIT 5 Routes of Drug Administration	24
UNIT 6 Administration Instructions	28
UNIT 7 Administration Details	32
UNIT 8 Learning Lab: How to Administer Medicine	36
UNIT 9 Precautions and Storage	40
UNIT 10 Learning Lab: Precautions and Storage	44
UNIT 11 Learning Lab: Precautions and Storage: Specialized Vocabulary	48
UNIT 12 Over-the-Counter Medicine Roleplay	52
UNIT 13 Prescription Medicine Roleplay	56
UNIT 14 Comprehensive Practice: Speaking	60
UNIT 15 Comprehensive Practice: Writing	62
Appendix	64

UNIT 1

Introduction to Explaining Medicine

When dispensing medicine, a pharmacist should explain four things: 1) what the medicine is; 2) how to administer the medicine; 3) precautions; and 4) storage methods.

1) What the medicine is

First, tell the patient what you are giving them. Explain: 1) the type of medicine (cold medicine, antibiotics, etc.)（薬の種類）; and 2) what it is effective for (indications).（効能・効果）

e.g. "This is <u>cold medicine</u>. It is for <u>fever and runny nose</u>."
　　　　　　（薬の種類）　　　　　　　（効能・効果）

2) How to administer the medicine

Next, inform the patient how to use the medicine. Include these five points: method of administration（投与方法）, dosage（用量）, frequency（頻度）, time of day（時間）, and duration（期間）.

e.g. "<u>Take</u> <u>one tablet</u>, <u>three times a day</u>, <u>after meals</u>, <u>for three days</u>."
　　　（投与方法）（用量）　　（頻度）　　　（時間）　　（期間）

3) Precautions

After that, discuss with the patient possible risks and concerns (precautions). Focus on these four points: adverse reactions / side effects（副作用）, restrictions on use（使用についての制限）, present illnesses and present conditions（現病歴と現在の状態）, and previous medical history（既応歴）.

e.g. "This medicine may cause <u>drowsiness</u>, so <u>do not drive after taking it</u>."
　　　　　　　　　　　　　　　（副作用）　　　　（使用についての制限）

"<u>Consult a doctor before taking this</u> if <u>you have asthma</u>."
　（使用についての制限）　　　　　　（現病歴）

"<u>Do not take this</u> if <u>you have had an allergic reaction caused by this medicine</u>."
（使用についての制限）　　　　　　　　（既応歴）

4) Storage methods

Finally, tell the patient how to store the medicine（保存方法）. Focus your explanation on:

a) things to keep the medicine "away from" (light, heat, children, etc.); and

b) places to keep the medicine (in a cool, dark place, the refrigerator, etc.).

e.g. "<u>Keep this away from direct sunlight, heat, and moisture</u>."
　　　　　　　　　　　（保存方法）

Comprehension Questions

1. What are the four main topics to cover when explaining medicine?

   _____

2. What are the key points of the "What the medicine is" explanation?

   _____

3. What are the key points of the "How to administer the medicine" explanation?

   _____

4. What are the key points of the "Precautions" explanation?

   _____

5. What are the key points of the "Storage methods" explanation?

   a) _____

   b) _____

Find the Errors

Find the errors and rewrite the following sentences.

1. Cold medicine is it. It is fever and runny nose.

   _____

2. One tablet is taking three times a day, after a meal.

   _____

3. Consult a doctor taking this before if you have asthma.

   _____

4. Keep this in direct sunlight, heat, and moisture.

   _____

Exercise 1

Match the words and phrases in the box with the explanation categories below. The first one is done for you.

a. Adverse reactions / side effects	**b.** Frequency	**c.** What it is effective for
d. Present illnesses and present conditions	**e.** How to store	**f.** Restrictions on use
g. Method of administration	**h.** Dosage	**i.** ~~Type of medicine~~
j. Previous medical history	**k.** Duration	**l.** Time of day

Part 1: What the medicine is

1. _____ i. Type of medicine _____

2. _____

Part 2: How to administer the medicine

3. _____

4. _____

5. _____

6. _____

7. _____

Part 3: Precautions

8. _____

9. _____

10. _____

11. _____

Part 4: Storage methods

12. _____

Exercise 2

Translate the sentences into English.

What the medicine is

1. これは風邪薬です。発熱と鼻水のための薬です。

   _____

How to administer the medicine

2. 3日間、1錠剤を1日3回食後に飲んでください。

   _____

Precautions

3. この薬は眠気を起こすかもしれませんので、車の運転をしないでください。

   _____

4. 喘息の方はこの薬の服用前に医者に相談してください。

   _____

5. この薬にアレルギー反応を起こしたことがある方はこの薬を服用しないでください。

   _____

Storage methods

6. 直射日光、高温多湿を避けてください。

   _____

UNIT 2

Types of Medicine: "What is this?"

Common Types of Medicine

In English, we can use the words "medicine," "medication" and, "drug" to describe various types of "医薬品." However, "medicine" or "medication" are used more commonly by people outside the medical profession. For example, "風邪薬" is "cold medicine" or "cold medication," not "cold drug."

Pharmacists should use everyday English, not specialized medical words, when explaining medicine. For example, words like "pain reliever" or "painkiller," are easier for patients to understand than "analgesic（鎮痛剤）."

A useful rule to explain medicine simply is: **a)** say the problem or place, then add the word "medicine" or **b)** say "medicine for" and the name of the disease.
e.g. cold medicine, stomach medicine, medicine for asthma, medicine for diabetes

Finally, there are some kinds of medicine that have specialized names, including eye drops, suppositories, lozenges, and laxatives. For this kind of medicine, do not add the word "medicine." For example: Do not say "eye drops medicine."

Comprehension Questions

1. What English word do most people use for "医薬品"?

   _____

2. What are two other English words for "analgesic"?

   _____

3. What is a rule for explaining medicine?

   a) _____

   b) _____

Vocabulary Lists

Below are some examples of medicines.

General 一般
- ☐ cold medicine — 風邪薬
- ☐ a pain reliever / a painkiller — 痛み止め・鎮痛薬
- ☐ antiviral medicine — 抗ウイルス薬
- ☐ an antibiotic / antibacterial medicine — 抗生物質
- ☐ anti-fever medicine — 解熱剤
- ☐ a suppository — 座薬
- ☐ a supplement — サプリメント
- ☐ allergy medicine — 抗アレルギー薬
- ☐ motion-sickness medicine / medicine for travel sickness — 酔い止め

Nose, throat and eyes 鼻、のど、眼
- ☐ a nasal spray — 点鼻用スプレー
- ☐ medicine for asthma — 喘息薬
- ☐ a gargle — うがい薬
- ☐ an inhalant — 吸入薬
- ☐ cough medicine — 咳止め
- ☐ cough drops — 薬用キャンディ
- ☐ lozenges — トローチ
- ☐ eye drops — 目薬

Gastrointestinal 消化器
- ☐ an antacid — 制酸薬
- ☐ stomach medicine — 胃腸薬
- ☐ a laxative — 便秘薬
- ☐ diarrhea medicine / medicine for diarrhea — 下痢止め

Skin 皮膚
- ☐ an ointment — 塗り薬
- ☐ an antiseptic — 消毒薬
- ☐ a patch — 湿布／パッチ

Other 他
- ☐ medicine for high blood pressure — 高血圧薬
- ☐ medicine for heart disease — 心臓病の薬
- ☐ medicine for diabetes / an antidiabetic — 糖尿病薬
- ☐ an antidepressant — 抗うつ剤

Exercise 1

Imagine you are working in a pharmacy. For each person below, what kind of medicine would you recommend? (More than one answer is possible!)

1. I have a cough.

   _____

2. I have really dry eyes.

   _____

3. I've cut my finger.

   _____

4. I have nasal allergies.

   _____

5. I'm going whale-watching in a boat after lunch.

   _____

6. I have diarrhea.

   _____

7. I have a cold.

   _____

Exercise 2

Write the English translations for each type of medicine in the matching places in the puzzle. The first one has been done for you.

Down
2. 坐薬
3. 風邪薬
4. 吸入薬
5. 塗り薬
7. 消毒薬
9. 湿布／パッチ

Across
1. 目薬
6. 便秘薬
7. 抗生物質
8. サプリメント

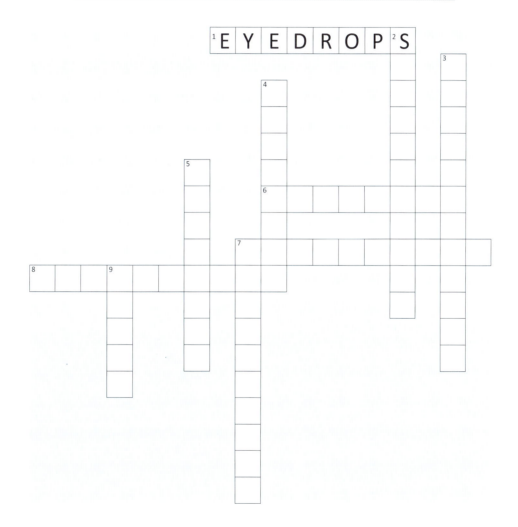

UNIT 3

Symptoms: "What is it for?"

Common Symptoms and Medical Conditions

In English, we mainly use "have" to describe symptoms or illnesses. For example, "I have a headache" or "I have a cold." We also sometimes use "feel" to describe tiredness, weakness, etc. For example, "I feel tired" or "I feel weak."

Finally, we use "be" to describe conditions such as "I am pregnant" or "I am dizzy."

Vocabulary Lists

Below are some commonly used words to describe symptoms.

General 一般

☐ an infection	感染症／化膿
☐ a fever	発熱
☐ chills	寒気
☐ inflammation	炎症
☐ swelling	腫れ
☐ a cold	風邪
☐ insomnia	不眠症
☐ influenza / the flu	インフルエンザ
☐ a hangover	二日酔い
☐ allergy / allergies	アレルギー
☐ allergic reaction	アレルギー反応
☐ weakness (feel weak)	脱力感
☐ tiredness (feel tired)	倦怠感
☐ drowsiness (feel drowsy)	眠気
☐ pain	痛み
☐ acute pain	急性疼痛
☐ chronic pain	慢性疼痛

Head 頭

☐ a headache	頭痛
☐ dizziness	めまい
☐ an earache / ear pain	耳痛
☐ ringing in the ears	耳なり

Nose, throat and eyes 鼻、のど、眼

☐ nasal allergies	鼻炎
☐ pollen allergies / hay fever	花粉症

14　Medication Explained　Essential English for Pharmacists

- ☐ a runny nose 鼻水
- ☐ a stuffy nose / nasal congestion 鼻づまり
- ☐ head congestion 頭重（感）
- ☐ phlegm たん
- ☐ a cough 咳
- ☐ a sore throat のどの痛み
- ☐ a swollen throat のどの腫れ
- ☐ asthma 喘息
- ☐ asthma attack 喘息発作
- ☐ trouble breathing 呼吸困難
- ☐ eye fatigue 眼精疲労
- ☐ eye pain 目の痛み
- ☐ dry eyes ドライアイ
- ☐ itchy eyes 目のかゆみ
- ☐ bloodshot eyes 充血
- ☐ glaucoma 緑内障
- ☐ a sty ものもらい
- ☐ pink eye / conjunctivitis 結膜炎
- ☐ watery eyes 涙目
- ☐ sneeze / sneezing くしゃみ

Mouth 口

- ☐ a toothache 歯痛
- ☐ a cavity 虫歯
- ☐ a canker sore 口内炎
- ☐ bleeding gums 歯茎の出血

Gastrointestinal 消化器

- ☐ nausea (feel nauseous) 吐き気
- ☐ vomiting 嘔吐
- ☐ diarrhea 下痢
- ☐ constipation 便秘
- ☐ heartburn 胸やけ
- ☐ indigestion 消化不良
- ☐ gas ガス（がたまる）
- ☐ hemorrhoids 痔
- ☐ weight loss , weight gain 体重減少，体重増加
- ☐ stomach flu / gastroenteritis 胃腸炎
- ☐ poor appetite 食欲不振
- ☐ stomachache / abdominal pain 胃痛／腹痛

Urinary 泌尿器

- ☐ urinary infection 尿路感染症
- ☐ painful urination 排尿痛

Skin 皮膚

- ☐ dermatitis — 皮膚炎
- ☐ rash — 発疹／かぶれ
    - ☐ diaper rash — おむつかぶれ
    - ☐ heat rash — あせも
- ☐ atopic dermatitis — アトピー性皮膚炎
- ☐ hives (common cause: food allergy) — 蕁麻疹
- ☐ eczema (common cause: environment) — 湿疹
- ☐ a burn — やけど
- ☐ a sunburn — 日焼け
- ☐ severe frostbite, mild frostbite — 凍傷，しもやけ
- ☐ dry skin — 乾燥
- ☐ chapped skin — あかぎれ
- ☐ cracked skin — ひび
- ☐ acne / pimples — にきび
- ☐ a blister — 水ぶくれ／まめ
- ☐ athlete's foot — 水虫
- ☐ dandruff — ふけ
- ☐ a cold sore — 口唇ヘルペス（単純ヘルペス）
- ☐ itchiness — かゆみ
- ☐ an insect bite — 虫さされ
- ☐ weeping sore / wet sore — ただれ

Chest 胸

- ☐ shortness of breath — 息切れ
- ☐ angina (chest pain) — 狭心症（胸痛）
- ☐ heart attack — 心臓発作
- ☐ high cholesterol — 高コレステロール
- ☐ high blood pressure, low blood pressure — 高血圧，低血圧

Obstetrics 婦人科

- ☐ period / menstruation — 生理
- ☐ menstrual cramps — 生理痛
- ☐ be pregnant — 妊娠中
- ☐ be breastfeeding — 授乳中

Other 他

- ☐ diabetes — 糖尿病
- ☐ blood sugar level — 血糖値
- ☐ a sprain — ねんざ
- ☐ a bruise — 打撲
- ☐ stiff muscles / muscle pain — こり／筋肉痛
- ☐ numbness — しびれ
- ☐ arthritis — 関節炎
- ☐ joint pain — 関節痛
- ☐ backache — 腰痛

Exercise 1

Write the symptoms and conditions in the matching places in the puzzle. The first one has been done for you.

Down
1. ~~a high temperature~~
2. when your skin freezes
3. to give milk to a baby
5. what you have after eating spicy food
7. similar to sleepiness

Across
4. dermatitis caused by food
5. dermatitis caused by sweat
6. the day after you drink too much
8. joint disease
9. a kind of chest pain

Unit 3   Symptoms: "What is it for?"

Exercise 2

Write the symptoms and conditions from the box on the lines below. The first one has been done for you.

~~pain~~	dry eyes	stuffy nose	stiff muscles	skin infections
cough	~~fever~~	indigestion	viral infections	runny nose
nausea	sore throat	constipation	itchy eyes	muscle pain

1. Pain reliever: It is for ____pain____ and ____fever____.

2. Motion-sickness medicine: It is for _____

3. Antiviral medicine: It is for _____

4. Antiseptic: It is for _____

5. Stomach medicine: It is for _____

6. Laxative: It is for _____

7. Cough medicine: It is for _____ and _____

8. Cold medicine: It is for cold symptoms, such as _____ and _____

9. Eye drops: They are for eye problems, such as _____ and _____

10. Patch: It is for _____ and _____

18   Medication Explained   Essential English for Pharmacists

Exercise 3

Translate the sentences into easy-to-understand English.

e.g. 鎮痛剤です。痛みを和らげ、熱を下げます。

_____This is a pain reliever. It is for pain and fever._____

1. 酔い止めの薬です。吐き気をおさえます。

   _____

2. うがい薬です。のどの痛みを和らげます。

   _____

3. 喘息の薬です。呼吸をしやすくします。

   _____

4. 点鼻用スプレーです。花粉症の症状を和らげます 。

   _____

5. 胃薬です。食物の消化を促します。

   _____

6. 水虫の塗り薬です。かゆみを止めます。

   _____

7. 抗生物質です。病気の原因菌を死滅させます。

   _____

8. 高血圧薬です。血圧を下げます。

   _____

9. 目薬です。目の疲れと痛みを和らげます。

   _____

UNIT 4

Learning Lab: Medicine Types and Purpose

Exercise 1

Explain the following medicines. Use the Appendix on p.64-70.

e.g. 抗生物質
- A) This is an antibiotic. / This is antibacterial medicine.
- B) It is for bacterial infections. / It is for fighting bacteria.

① 坐薬
- A) _____
- B) _____

② うがい液
- A) _____
- B) _____

③ インスリン
- A) _____
- B) _____

④ ロートアルガード® コンタクト a
- A) _____
- B) _____

⑤ ユースキン Aa

　　A) _____

　　B) _____

⑥ ロートアルガード ®ST 鼻炎スプレー

　　A) _____

　　B) _____

⑦ パブロン鼻炎カプセル S α

　　A) _____

　　B) _____

⑧ ナロンエース T

　　A) _____

　　B) _____

＊骨折痛：bone fracture pain，＊神経痛：nerve pain

⑨ パブロンゴールド A〈微粒〉

　　A) _____

　　B) _____

Medicine for Specific Body Parts

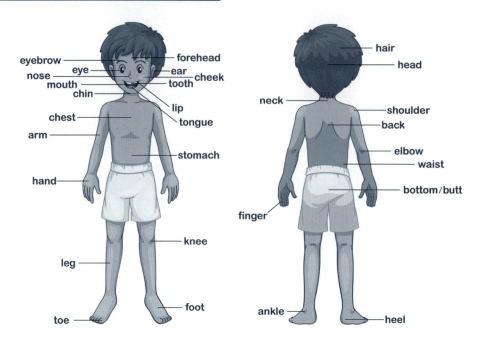

Exercise 2

Imagine you are working in a pharmacy. For each person below, what kind of medicine would you recommend and what are the effects?

e.g. I have a toothache.

          This is a pain reliever. It is for pain and fever.

1. I have a stiff shoulder.

   _____

2. I have acne on his forehead.

   _____

3. I have a cut on his finger.

   _____

4. I have a sty in his eye.

   _____

5. I have athlete's foot.

   _____

6. I have a sprained ankle.

   _____

Exercise 3

Write English translations for each body parts in the matching places in the puzzle. The first one has been done for you.

Down	Across
1. ~~腰~~	3. 足首
2. 首	5. 胸
4. ひじ	7. 尻
6. 舌	8. 足の指
9. ひざ	10. 額

UNIT 5

Routes of Drug Administration

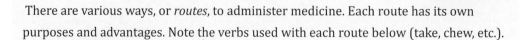

There are various ways, or *routes*, to administer medicine. Each route has its own purposes and advantages. Note the verbs used with each route below (take, chew, etc.).

1) **Oral Route**（経口ルート）

   Patients "take" medicine through the mouth. Sometimes patients "chew" medicine before swallowing. The oral route is the most commonly used route because it is easy and convenient.

2) **Sublingual Route**（舌下ルート）

   Patients "put" medicine under the tongue to melt it. Sublingual medicine is used when a rapid onset is needed, such as medicine for heart disease and motion sickness.

3) **Inhalation Route**（吸入ルート）

   Patients "inhale" the medicine through the mouth or "spray" medicine in the nose. Inhalants are used for nasal or respiratory problems, such as medicine for allergies and asthma.

4) **Topical Route**（局部ルート）

   Patients "apply" medicine, "put" medicine on/in the affected area（患部）, "gargle" medicine, or "suck on" medicine (cough drops). Topical medicine is used when a local effect is needed.

5) **Rectal Route and Vaginal Route**（直腸ルート・膣ルート）

   Patients "insert" suppositories into the anus or vagina. A suppository is usually used for people who cannot take medicine orally, such as infants or elderly people.

6) **Injection Route**（注射ルート）

   Some patients "inject" medicine just below the skin or in the muscle. Subcutaneous administration（皮下投与）and intramuscular administration（筋肉内投与）are often used for insulin treatment or in response to an anaphylactic reaction.

Comprehension Questions

1. **A)** What are the advantages of the oral route?
   _____

   B) How is it administered?
   _____

2. **A)** When do we use the sublingual route?
   _____

   B) Where is it administered?
   _____

3. **A)** What kind of problems is the inhalation route used for?
   _____

   B) How is it administered?
   _____

4. **A)** When do we use the topical route?
   _____

   B) Where is it administered?
   _____

5. **A)** Why are suppositories used for children and elderly people?
   _____

   B) How are they administered?
   _____

6. **A)** What is the injection route used for?
   _____

   B) Where is it injected?
   _____

Exercises

Imagine you are working in a pharmacy. For each person below, suggest a medicine for each complaint below. Use the correct verb for each route as shown in the example.

e.g. I have a cold.

_____Take cold medicine._____

1. I have a rash.

   _____

2. My one-year-old child has a fever.

   _____

3. I have nausea when I go driving.

   _____

4. I have nasal allergies caused by pollen.

   _____

5. I have asthma.

   _____

6. I have a headache.

   _____

7. I have dry eyes.

   _____

8. I have influenza.

_____

9. I have diabetes.

_____

10. I have a cough.

_____

11. I have a stiff shoulder.

_____

12. I have an itchy mosquito bite.

_____

13. I have constipation.

_____

14. I have a cut on my finger.

_____

UNIT 6

Administration Instructions

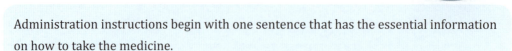

Administration instructions begin with one sentence that has the essential information on how to take the medicine.

e.g. "Take two tablets, three times a day after meals for a week."

Method of administration (投与方法)	Start with a verb.	Take
Dosage (用量)	Tell how much.	two tablets
Frequency (頻度)	Tell how often.	three times a day
Time of day (時間)	Tell the time of day.	after meals
Duration (期間)	Tell how many days.	for a week

1) Always say the method of administration, dosage and frequency together. Do not separate them!
2) Time of day is almost always needed.
3) Be sure to specify duration with antibacterial and antiviral medicines.

Vocabulary Lists

Below are commonly used vocabulary when giving administration instructions.

Method (方法)

- ☐ apply / put ~ on　　　　　〜を…に貼る／塗る
- ☐ gargle　　　　　　　　　うがいをする
- ☐ inhale　　　　　　　　　吸入する
- ☐ inject　　　　　　　　　注射する
- ☐ insert / put ~ in　　　　　〜を…に入れる
- ☐ chew　　　　　　　　　噛んで飲む
- ☐ put ~ under　　　　　　〜を…の下に入れる
- ☐ suck on　　　　　　　　なめる
- ☐ spray　　　　　　　　　スプレーする・噴霧する
- ☐ take　　　　　　　　　　飲む
- ☐ swallow　　　　　　　　飲みこむ

Dosage (用量)

- ☐ capsule　　　　　　　　カプセル
- ☐ tablet　　　　　　　　　錠剤
- ☐ packet　　　　　　　　　小さな包み

- ☐ measurement 目盛り
- ☐ suppository 坐薬
- ☐ patch 湿布／パッチ
- ☐ inhalation 吸入
- ☐ lozenge / cough drop トローチ／薬用キャンディ・のどあめ
- ☐ drop 滴
- ☐ adequate amount of ~ 適量
  (If a patient asks "How much is enough?"
  You can answer "About one or two (or more) fingertips of ointment.")
- ☐ ~ this ~ times これを〜回
  - ☐ Spray this twice. これを2回スプレーしてください。
  - ☐ Inhale this three times. これを3回吸入してください。
- ☐ ~ this as directed by your doctor
  (the amount directed by your doctor) 医師の指示通り

Frequency（頻度）
- ☐ ~ times a day 1日〜回
  - ☐ once a day 1日1回
  - ☐ several times a day 1日数回
- ☐ every ~ 毎〜／〜ごと
  - ☐ every two hours 2時間ごと
  - ☐ every day 毎日
- ☐ When you have ~ 〜のある時
  - ☐ When you have pain 痛みのある時
  - ☐ When you have nausea 吐き気のある時

Time of day（時間）
- ☐ in the ~ 〜中／〜に
  - ☐ in the morning 午前中
  - ☐ in the evening 夕方に
- ☐ before ~ 〜の前
  - ☐ before meals 食前
  - ☐ before bedtime 寝る前
  - ☐ one hour before bedtime 寝る1時間前
- ☐ after ~ 〜の後
  - ☐ after meals 食後
  - ☐ after you eat something 何かを食べた後
- ☐ within (time) 〜時間内
  - ☐ within 30 minutes after meals 食後30分以内

Duration（期間）
- ☐ for (time) 〜日分の薬
  - ☐ for five days 5日間分
  - ☐ for two weeks 2週間分

Exercises

Translate the sentences into English. Follow the example.

Oral Medicine

e.g. 2/3 包を 1 日 3 回食後に飲んでください。

_____Take two thirds of a packet three times a day after meals._____

1. 1 錠を 1 日 2 回朝夕食後に服用してください。

   _____

2. 1 包を 1 日 1 回寝る前服用してください。5 日分の薬です。

   _____

3. 1 カプセルを痛みのある時に服用してください。

   _____

Sublingual Medicine

4. 車酔いによるめまいのある時 1 錠を噛んで服用してください。

   _____

Topical Medicine

5. 患部に１日数回塗ってください。

___

Suppository

6. 高熱時に肛門に１個を挿入してください。

___

Inhalant

7. 喘息発作時に１回吸入してください。

___

8. 花粉症の症状のある時１回鼻に噴霧してください。

___

Injection Medicine

9. アナフィラキシー反応を起こした時１回太腿に注射を行ってください。

___

* アナフィラキシー反応：anaphylactic reaction　　太腿筋：the thigh muscle

UNIT 7
Administration Details

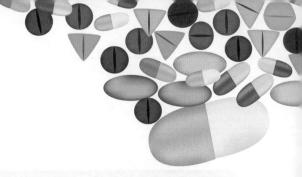

Unit 6 covered the specific instruction on how to administer medicine. Next, it is time to give extra details, such as what to do before, during or after using the medicine, dosage limits and age considerations for children or elderly patients.

1) Non-oral medicine (飲み薬以外)

Do not take this orally. / Do not take this by mouth.
(口から使用しないでください。)

Do not swallow this. （飲み込むな。）　＊主にうがい薬と噛んで飲む薬についての表現

2) Activities before, during, and after use (使用前、使用中、使用後)

a. ... before using this (使用する前に〜)

Clean the affected area before using this.
(使用する前に患部をきれいにしてください。)

Shake well before using this.
(使用する前によく振ってください。)

Mix 5 drops with 100 ml of water before using this.
Put 5 drops in 100 ml of water before using this.
(使用する前に5滴を100mlの水に入れてください。)

b. ... after using this (使用した後に〜)

Gargle after using this.
(使用した後うがいをしてください。)

c. ... while/when using this (使用している時に〜)

Do not drink when using this.
(使用中アルコールを飲まないでください。)

3) **Dosage limits**（用量の制限）

   a. **Wait ... hours between doses.**（〜時間空けて服用してください）
      Wait four hours between doses.
      Take doses four hours apart.
      （4時間空けて服用してください。）

   b. **Do not ... more than ... times a day.**（1日〜回まで／1日〜回限度）
      Do not take this more than three times a day.
      （この薬は1日3回まで／1日3回限度）

4) **With ...**（〜と一緒に）

   Take this with a glass of water.
   （コップ一杯の水で飲んでください。）

   Do not take this with grapefruit juice.
   （グレープフルーツジュースで飲まないでください。）

5) **Age**（年齢制限）

   a. **Children age ... and older**（〜才以上の子ども）
      Children age 7 and older shoud take one packet.
      （7才以上の子どもは1回1包を服用してください。）

   b. **Children ages A to B**（A才からB才の子ども）
      Children ages 3 to 6 should take a half of a packet.
      （3才から6才の子どもは1回1/2包を服用してください。）

   c. **Children under age ...**（〜才未満の子ども）
      Children under age 3 should not take this.
      （3才未満の子どもは服用しないこと。）
      Children age 2 and younger should not take this.
      （2才以下の子どもは服用しないこと。）

Explaining partial doses（分数の読み方）

一包の　　1/2: half of a packet
　　　　　1/3: one third of a packet
　　　　　2/3: two thirds of a packet
　　　　　1/4: one fourth of a packet / one quarter of a packet
　　　　　3/4: three fourths of a packet / three quarters of a packet

Exercises

Translate the sentences into English. Follow the example.

e.g. 坐薬です。飲んではいけません。

_____This is a suppository. Do not take this orally._____

1. 使用する前に手を洗ってください。

   _____

2. 15 才以上の方は 1 包を 1 日 1 回寝る前に服用してください。

   _____

3. 7 才から 14 才の子どもは 2/3 包を服用してください。

   _____

4. 7 才未満の子どもは服用しないこと。

   _____

5. 6 時間空けて服用してください。

   _____

6. 1日3回を限度。

___

7. この薬を使用中授乳しないでください。

___

8. コップ一杯のぬるま湯で飲んでください。

___

9. コンタクトレンズを外して点眼してください。

___

Hint：before

Bonus 服薬中も授乳を続けてもかまいません。

___

UNIT 8

Learning Lab: How to Administer Medicine

Exercises

Explain the following medicines. Use the Appendix on p.64-70.

e.g. 抗生物質　Oral Route

C) ___Take one tablet, once a day, after breakfast, for seven days.___

① 坐薬　Rectal Route

C) _____

D) _____

　　　　　　　　　　　　　　　　　　　Hint：口から使用しないでください

② うがい液　Topical Route

C) _____

D) then _____

E) _____

　　　　　　　　　　　　　　　　　　　　　　　Hint：飲み込むな

③ インスリン　Injection Route

C) _____

36　Medication Explained　Essential English for Pharmacists

④ ロートアルガード®コンタクトa　Topical Route

C) _____

⑤ ユースキンAa　Topical Route

C) _____

D) _____

⑥ ロートアルガード®ST鼻炎スプレー　Inhalation Route

C) _____
　　　　　　　　　　　　　　　　Hint：両鼻腔内に→それぞれの鼻孔（each nostril）に

D) _____

E) _____

F) _____

Good Practice Note

Some things are not always written in Japanese, but they are important to tell patients. For example, on page 64, these sentences are not written:

口から使用しないでください　or　飲み込むな

However, here the pharmacist says them to improve understanding.

⑦ パブロン鼻炎カプセルＳα　Oral Route

C) _____

D) _____

E) _____

F) _____

⑧ ナロンエースＴ　Oral Route

C) _____

D) _____

E) _____

F) _____

G) _____

⑨ パブロンゴールドＡ〈微粒〉　Oral Route

C) _____

D) _____

E) _____

F) _____

MEMO

UNIT 9

Precautions and Storage

Precautions

There are many precautions to discuss before dispensing any medicine. Here we will examine four points.

1) Adverse reactions / side effects (副作用)

This medicine may cause ... （この薬は〜を起こすかもしれない）
This medicine may cause dizziness.
You may have dizziness when taking this.
（この薬はめまいを起こすかもしれません。）

2) Restrictions on use （使用についての制限）

a. Be careful ... （〜に注意してください）

Be (very) careful driving or operating machines after taking this.
（服用後、車の運転や機械類の操作をする時は（十分に）注意してください。）

b. Do not ... （〜しないでください）

Do not drive or operate machines after taking this.
（服用後、車の運転や機械類の操作をしないでください。）

c. You must ... （必ず〜してください）

You must finish taking all of this medicine even if your symptoms disappear.
（症状が消えてもすべての薬を最後まで飲んでください。）
（途中で服用を絶対に止めないでください。）

d. You must not ... （絶対に〜してはいけません）

You must not take this medicine with any other pain relievers.
（この薬は絶対に他の鎮痛薬と一緒に飲んではいけません。）

3) **Present illnesses and present conditions**（現病歴と現在の状態）

   a. if you have (condition)　（［現病歴］があれば）
      Consult a doctor before taking this if you have asthma.
      Speak with a doctor before taking this if you have asthma.
      （喘息があればこの薬を服用前に医師に相談してください。）

   b. if you are (condition)　（［～］している場合／［現在の状態］ならば）
      Consult a doctor before taking this if you are pregnant.
      Speak with a doctor before taking this if you are pregnant.
      （妊娠している場合この薬を服用前に医師に相談してください。）

4) **Previous medical history**（既応歴）

   a. if you have had (... reaction)　（［有害反応］を起こしたことがあれば）
      Do not take this if you have had an allergic reaction caused by this medicine.
      （この薬にアレルギー反応を起こしたことがあったら、この薬を服用しないでください。）

Storage

Explain the best storage environment, including specific things to avoid that may affect the medicine.

   a. Keep this away from ...　（～から離しておく）
      Keep this away from direct sunlight, heat and moisture.
      （直射日光、高温多湿を避けてください。）
      Keep this away from children.
      （子どもの手が届かない所に保存してください。）

   b. Keep this in ...　（～に保管する）
      Keep this in the refrigerator.
      （冷蔵庫で保存してください。）

Exercises

Translate the sentences into English. Follow the example.

e.g. この薬は眠気を起こすかもしれないので、車の運転には注意してください。

_____This medicine may cause drowsiness, so be careful driving._____

1. この薬の服用中便秘になる可能性があります。

   _____

2. この薬は胃に負担がかかる（胃の不調を起こす）ことがあります。

   _____

3. この薬をほかの鎮痛剤と一緒に使用しないでください。

   _____

4. この薬をかぶれがある部位には塗らないでください。

   _____

5. 途中で服用を絶対に止めないでください。

   _____

6. 卵アレルギーの方はこの薬の服用前に医師に相談してください。

   _____

7. 妊娠中の方はこの薬を服用しないでください。

   _____

8. 本剤によってアレルギー症状を起こしたことがある人は使用しないでください。

   _____

9. この薬は冷蔵庫で保存してください。

   _____

Bonus　アレルギー体質の人は服用前に医師に相談してください。

   _____

UNIT 10

Learning Lab: Precautions and Storage

Exercises

Explain the following medicines. Use the Appendix on p.64-70.

e.g. 抗生物質

D) This medicine may cause a rash or stomach troubles such as nausea, vomiting, and diarrhea.

E) You must finish taking all of your medicine even if your symptoms disappear.

_{* See Good Practice Note on page 46.}

① 坐薬

E) _____

F) _____

* 体温：temperature

② うがい液

F) _____

③ インスリン

D) _____

_____

* 低血糖：low blood sugar　　アナフィラキシーショック：anaphylactic shock

Hint：血管神経性浮腫→まぶたや唇の腫れ，じんましん

④ ロートアルガード® コンタクト a

D) _____

   （1）_____

   （2）_____

   （3）_____

   （4）_____

E) _____

⑤ ユースキン Aa

E) _____
                                                              ＊湿潤：damp skin

F) _____

G) _____
                                                              ＊発赤：redness

H) _____

I) _____

J) _____

⑥ ロートアルガード®ST 鼻炎スプレー

G) _____

H) _____

   （1）_____

   （2）_____

   （3）_____

   （4）_____

   （5）_____

                                                ＊甲状腺機能障害：thyroid disease

   （6）_____

I) _____

Good Practice Note

Some precautions are not always written in Japanese, but they are important to tell the patients. For example, on page 64, this sentence is not written: 症状が消えてもすべての薬を最後まで飲んでください However, for the antibiotics on page 44 the pharmacist says it to help prevent drug resistance.

MEMO

Unit 11

Learning Lab: Precautions and Storage: Specialized Vocabulary

Specialized Vocabulary

Some kinds of medicine use specialized vocabulary in the precautions. For example, some kinds of medicine list the condition 「前立腺肥大」, which is "benign prostatic hyperplasia." For most people, that is not easily understood. So, the pharmacist needs to find a way to simplify it.

A useful rule to explain specialized vocabulary for medical conditions is to say:
body part and disorder/problem/disease
e.g. a prostate disorder / a prostate problem / prostate disease

Comprehension Questions

1. Why is "benign prostatic hyperplasia" not the best choice to use for explaining medicine?

   _____

2. What is the rule for explaining specialized vocabulary?

   _____

Exercises

Explain the following medicines. Use the Appendix on p.64-70.

⑦ パブロン鼻炎カプセル S α

G) _____

  (1) _____
                                                                                   * 成分：active ingredient

  (2) _____

  (3) _____

H) _____

I) _____

  (1) _____

  (2) _____

  (3) _____

  (4) _____

  (5) _____

  (6) _____
                              Hint：鎮咳去痰薬→たんの薬　　鼻炎用内服薬→鼻炎の薬

  (7) _____

  (8) _____
                                                                                     * 腎臓病：kidney disease

  (9) _____
                * モノアミン酸化酵素阻害剤（セレギリン塩酸塩）：monoamine oxidase inhibitors

J) _____

K) _____

L) _____
                                                                                     * 使用期限：expiration date

⑧ ナロンエース T

H) _____

   (1) _____

   (2) _____

   (3) _____

   (4) _____
                                           * 出産予定日 12 週以内：within 12 weeks of delivery

I) _____

J) _____

   (1) _____

   (2) _____

   (3) _____

   (4) _____

   (5) _____

   (6) _____
                                           * 肝臓病：liver disease
        Hint：全身性エリテマトーデス，混合性結合組織病→自己免疫疾患：autoimmune disease

   (7) _____
        Hint：胃・十二指腸潰瘍，潰瘍性大腸炎，クローン病→胃腸疾患：gastrointestinal disease

K) _____

L) _____

M) _____

⑨ パブロンゴールド A〈微粒〉

G) _____

   （1）_____

   （2）_____

H) _____

I) _____

J) _____

   （1）_____

   （2）_____

   （3）_____

   （4）_____

   （5）_____

   （6）_____

* 胃・十二指腸潰瘍：stomach disease, intestinal disease
呼吸機能障害：breathing disorder
閉塞性睡眠時無呼吸症候群：sleep disorder

K) _____

L) _____

M) _____

UNIT 12

Over-the-Counter Medicine Roleplay

Dialogue

A: Pharmacist, B: Customer

A: May I help you?
B: Yes. I have a terrible headache.
A: I'm sorry to hear that. How long have you had it?
B: Since this morning.
A: I see. Are you currently taking any medicine?
B: No.
A: Okay. Do you have any allergies to food or medicine?
B: No.
A: Are you pregnant or is there a possibility that you are pregnant?
B: Yes, I am three months pregnant.
A: I see. This is a pain reliever which pregnant women can take.

Comprehension Questions

1. What is the customer's problem?

   _____

2. Write the sentence that means, それは大変ですね。

   _____

3. How long has the customer had the headache?

   _____

4. What other medicine is the customer taking?

   _____

5. What problems in her previous medical history has she had?

   _____

6. What is the customer's present condition?

   _____

7. What kind of medicine does the pharmacist recommend?

   _____

Practice 1

Take turns with a partner practicing the conversation.
Student A (pharmacist): Ask the following questions in English.
Student B (customer): Look at the previous page and give hints to student A.

A: Pharmacist, B: Customer

A: どうしましたか？
B: I have a terrible headache.
A: それは大変ですね。いつからですか？
B: Since this morning.
A: I see. 現在服用している薬はありますか？
B: No.
A: Okay. 食べ物や薬などでアレルギー反応を起こしたことがありますか？
B: No.
A: 妊娠していますか、もしくはその可能性はありますか？
B: Yes, I am three months pregnant.
A: I see. This is 妊婦さんが飲んでも良い鎮痛剤 .

Practice 2

Practice a new conversation. The customer is taking another medicine. Use the following question.

A: I see. 現在服用している薬はありますか？
B: Yes.
A: Can you tell me the name of the medicine?
（薬の名前を教えていただけますか？）
B: Yes, it is ABC Multivitamin Supplement.

Writing

Write a conversation between a pharmacist and a customer with a cold. The customer has had a previous allergic reaction to medicine. Use the following questions in your conversation.

A: Okay. 食べ物や薬などでアレルギー反応を起こしたことがありますか？
B: Yes, once I had an allergic reaction to medicine.
A: 薬の名前を教えていただけますか？
B: No, but it was an antibiotic.
A: What happened when you took that medicine?
（その薬を飲んだ時どんなことが起こりましたか？）
B: I had a slight rash.
A: I see.

UNIT 13

Prescription Medicine Roleplay

Dialogue

A: Pharmacist, B: Patient

A: May I help you?
B: Yes. I have a prescription from Dr. Tanaka.
A: Okay. Please show me your prescription. Is this your first visit here?
B: Yes.
A: Could you show me your health insurance card?
B: Sorry, I forgot it.
A: If you do not have your health insurance card, you must pay the full fee.
B: Oh well.
A: Please fill out this questionnaire.
B: Sure.
A: Please have a seat and wait until your name is called.
B: Okay.

....

A: Medicine explanation here:
   (What the medicine is)
   (How to administer the medicine)
   (Precautions)
   (Storage methods)

....

A: The total comes to 2,932 yen. How would you like to pay?
B: By cash.
A: Here is your change and receipt.

Comprehension Questions

1. Does the man want OTC or prescription medicine?

   _____

2. How many times has he been to the pharmacy?

   _____

3. What did he forget at home?

   _____

4. Without the item from Question 3, what does he have to do?

   _____

5. What does he have to fill out?

   _____

6. What will he do while the pharmacist is preparing the medicine?

   _____

Unit 13   Prescription Medicine Roleplay   57

Practice 1

Take turns with a partner practicing the conversation.
Student A (pharmacist): Ask the following questions in English.
Student B (patient): Look at the previous page and give hints to student A.

> A: Pharmacist, B: Patient
>
> **A:** どうしましたか？
> **B:** I have a prescription from Dr. Tanaka.
> **A:** 処方箋を見せてください。こちらは初めてですか？
> **B:** Yes.
> **A:** 健康保険証を見せていただけますか？
> **B:** Sorry, I forgot it.
> **A:** 保険証をお持ちでない場合は全額負担となります。
> **B:** Oh well.
> **A:** この用紙に記入してください。
> **B:** Sure.
> **A:** 名前が呼ばれるまで、座ってお待ちください。
> **B:** Okay.
> ....
> **A:** Medicine explanation here:
>   (What the medicine is)
>   (How to administer the medicine)
>   (Precautions)
>   (Storage methods)
> ....
> **A:** 2,932 円になります。支払い方法はどうされますか？
> **B:** By cash.
> **A:** お釣りと領収書をどうぞ。

Practice 2

Practice a new conversation using this sentence:

> It should take about 40 minutes. You can wait here or come back later.
> （40 分ぐらいかかります。こちらで待っても良いですし、後で取りに来ても結構です。）

Writing

Write a conversation between a parent and a pharmacist. The prescription is for medicine for his/her young son. Use the following situation and question in your conversation.

B: I have a prescription for my son from Dr. Tanaka.

A: Can your son take tablets?（お子さんは錠剤が飲めますか？）

UNIT 14

Comprehensive Practice: Speaking

Role play Performance

With a partner, practice the dialogue. Then perform it in front of the teacher using the Performance Help Sheet.

A: Pharmacist, B: Customer

A: May I help you?
B: Yes. I have a headache.
A: I'm sorry to hear that. How long have you had it?
B: Since this morning.
A: I see. Do you have any allergies to food or medicine?
B: No.
A: Are you currently taking any medicine?
B: No.
A: Here you are. This is a pain reliever. It is for pain and fever.
B: Okay.
A: Take two tablets when you have pain, after you eat something. But do not take this more than three times a day, and wait four hours between doses. Finally, children under age 15 should not take this. Do you have a question?
B: No.
A: Before you take it, there are some precautions. First, this medicine may cause sleepiness, so do not drive or operate machines after taking it. Next, do not take this if you have had any allergic reactions or asthma attacks caused by pain relievers, anti-fever medicine or cold medicine. Do not take this if you are pregnant or there is a possibility that you are pregnant. Finally, keep this away from direct sunlight, heat, and moisture.
B: Okay.
A: The total comes to 2,932 yen. How would you like to pay?
B: By cash.
A: Here is your change and receipt.

※特定の OTC 薬ではなく一般的な事例の紹介です。

Performance Help Sheet

①どうしましたか？
　大変ですね・いつから？
　アレルギー反応は？
　服用している薬は？

②どうぞ
　鎮痛剤　痛みと熱
　2錠・痛みのある時・何かを食べた後
　3回を限度
　4時間あけて
　最後に・15歳未満

③注意
　First, 眠気 so 運転禁止
　Next, アレルギー反応または喘息発作
　Finally, 直射日光、熱、湿気を避けて

④支払い
　2,932円
　支払い方法は？
　お釣りと領収書

UNIT 15

Comprehensive Practice: Writing

Writing

A mother is going to take her children (ages 12 and 8) on a long drive.
Write the conversation between the mother and the pharmacist. Use the following medicine:

≪パッケージの記載≫

第２類医薬品

販売名：センパア QT〈ジュニア〉
（協力：大正製薬株式会社）

【効能】
　乗物酔いによるめまい・吐き気・頭痛の予防及び緩和

【用法・用量】
　次の量を口中で溶かして服用してください。
　乗物酔いの予防には乗車船 30 分前に１回量を服用します。
　なお、必要に応じて追加服用する場合には、１回量を４時間以上の間隔をおき服用してください。

11～14才	5～10才	5才未満
１回２錠	１回１錠	服用しないこと
１日２回まで	１日２回まで	

【注意】
　１．服用後、乗物又は機械類の運転操作をしないでください。
　２．次の人は服用前に医師、薬剤師又は登録販売者に相談してください。
　　（１）医師の治療を受けている人。
　　（２）妊婦又は妊娠していると思われる人。
　　（３）高齢者。
　　（４）薬などによりアレルギー症状を起こしたことがある人。
　　（５）次の症状のある人。　　排尿困難
　　（６）次の診断を受けた人。　　緑内障、心臓病
　３．服用に際しては、説明書をよく読んでください。
　４．直射日光の当たらない湿気の少ない涼しい所に保管してください。
　５．小児の手の届かない所に保管してください。
　６．使用期限を過ぎた製品は服用しないでください。

May I help you?

Appendix

e.g. A) 抗生物質

 白色の錠剤です。	起床	朝	昼	夜	寝前	B) 細菌による感染症の治療に用いる薬です。	D) 主な副作用は、発疹、吐き気、嘔吐、胃部不快感、腹部膨満感、腹痛、下痢等です。
		1					
	C) 1日1回 朝食後　7日分 （1日分1錠）						

① A) 坐薬

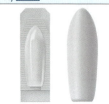	C) (頓) 肛門 38度以上の発熱時に使用のこと。	B) この薬は、熱を下げたり、炎症を起こしている部位の痛みを和らげます。	E) 他の解熱剤と一緒に使用しないでください。 F) 体温が下がりすぎた場合には、体をあたためてください。

② A) うがい液

	D) 1日数回 C) 1回5～7滴を約100mlの水に入れてうがいしてください。	B) のどや口の中の炎症を抑え、粘膜の炎症を抑えるうがい薬です。	F) 光、熱を避けてください。

③ A) インスリン

	C) 毎食前に医師から指示された量を皮下注射してください。	B) 血糖値を下げるインスリンの注射薬です。	D) 主な副作用は、低血糖（めまい、脱力、空腹感、冷や汗など）、アナフィラキシーショック（呼吸困難、ふらつきなど）、血管神経性浮腫（まぶたや、くちびるの腫れ、じんましんなど）

Appendix

④ A) 目薬

販売名：ロートアルガード® コンタクト a
（協力：ロート製薬株式会社）

≪パッケージの記載≫
【効能・効果】
　B) 目のかゆみ、目の疲れ、眼病予防（水泳のあと、ほこりや汗が目に入ったときなど）、紫外線その他の光線による眼炎（雪目など）、ソフトコンタクトレンズ又はハードコンタクトレンズを装着しているときの不快感、目のかすみ（目やにの多いときなど）

【用法・用量】
　C) 1回1～2滴、1日5～6回点眼してください。

【注意】
　1．D) 次の人は使用前に医師、薬剤師又は登録販売者にご相談ください。
　　（1）医師の治療を受けている人
　　（2）薬などによりアレルギー症状を起こしたことがある人
　　（3）次の症状のある人…はげしい目の痛み
　　（4）次の診断を受けた人…緑内障
　2．使用に際しては、説明書をよくお読みください。
　3．E) 直射日光の当たらない、涼しい所に密栓して保管してください。

Appendix

⑤ A) 塗り薬

指定医薬部外品
販売名：ユースキン Aa
（協力：ユースキン製薬株式会社）

【効能】
　B) ひび、あかぎれ、しもやけ

【使用法】
　D) 患部を清潔にしてから、C) １日数回適量をよくすり込んでください。

【使用上の注意】
　してはいけないこと
　（守らないと現在の症状が悪化したり、副作用が起こりやすくなります）
　（１）E) 次の人は使用しないでください。
　　　　湿潤やただれのひどい人

　相談すること
　（１）F) 次の人は使用前に医師、薬剤師または登録販売者にご相談ください。
　　　　薬や化粧品などによりアレルギー症状を起こしたことがある人
　（２）G) 使用後、次の症状があらわれた場合は副作用の可能性があるので、ただちに使用を中止し、この箱を持って医師、薬剤師または登録販売者にご相談ください。
　　　　関係部位：皮ふ　　症状：発疹・発赤、かゆみ

【保管及び取扱い上の注意】
　１．H) お子様の手の届かない所に保管してください。
　２．I) 直射日光をさけ、なるべく涼しい所にキャップをきちんとしめて保管してください。
　３．J) 他の容器に入れ替えないでください。
　　　　（誤用の原因になったり、品質が変わることがあります。）

Appendix

⑥ A) 鼻炎スプレー

販売名：ロートアルガード®ST 鼻炎スプレー
（協力：ロート製薬株式会社）

≪パッケージの記載≫
【効能】
B) 花粉、ハウスダスト（室内塵）などによる次のような鼻のアレルギー症状の緩和
鼻みず（鼻汁過多）、鼻づまり、くしゃみ、頭重（頭が重い）

【用法・用量】
D) 7才以上： C) 1回に1度ずつ、1日3～5回両鼻腔内に噴霧してください。なお、
E) 3時間以上の間隔をおいてください。
F) 3日間使用しても症状の改善がみられない場合には使用を中止し、医師又は薬剤師にご相談ください。

【注意】
1． G) 使用後、乗物又は機械類の運転操作をしないでください。
2． H) 次の人は使用前に医師、薬剤師又は登録販売者にご相談ください。
　　（1）医師の治療を受けている人
　　（2）妊婦又は妊娠していると思われる人
　　（3）薬などによりアレルギー症状を起こしたことがある人
　　（4）減感作療法等、アレルギーの治療を受けている人
　　（5）次の診断を受けた人
　　　　高血圧、心臓病、糖尿病、甲状腺機能障害、緑内障
　　（6）アレルギーによる症状か他の原因による症状かはっきりしない人
3．使用に際しては、説明書をよくお読みください。
4． I) 直射日光の当たらない涼しい所に密栓して保管してください。

Appendix

⑦ A) 鼻炎薬

 販売名：パブロン鼻炎カプセルSα
（協力：大正製薬株式会社）

≪パッケージの記載≫
【効能】
　B) 急性鼻炎、アレルギー性鼻炎又は副鼻腔炎による次の諸症状の緩和
　　くしゃみ、鼻みず（鼻汁過多）、鼻づまり、なみだ目、のどの痛み、頭重（頭が重い）

【用法・用量】
次の量を E) 12 時間ごとに D) 水又はぬるま湯で服用してください。

年令	1回量	服用回数
C) 15 才以上	C) 2 カプセル	C) 1日2回
F) 15 才未満　服用しないこと		

【注意】
1．G) 次の人は服用しないでください。
　（1）本剤又は本剤の成分によりアレルギー症状を起こしたことがある人。
　（2）次の症状のある人。
　　　前立腺肥大による排尿困難
　（3）次の診断を受けた人。
　　　高血圧、心臓病、甲状腺機能障害、糖尿病
2．H) 服用後、乗物又は機械類の運転操作をしないでください。
3．I) 次の人は服用前に医師、薬剤師又は登録販売者に相談してください。
　（1）医師の治療を受けている人。
　（2）妊婦又は妊娠していると思われる人。
　（3）授乳中の人。
　（4）高齢者。
　（5）薬などによりアレルギー症状を起こしたことがある人。
　（6）かぜ薬、鎮咳去痰薬、鼻炎用内服薬等により、不眠、めまい、脱力感、震え、動悸を起こしたことがある人。
　（7）次の症状のある人。
　　　高熱、排尿困難
　（8）次の診断を受けた人。
　　　緑内障、腎臓病
　（9）モノアミン酸化酵素阻害剤（セレギリン塩酸塩等）で治療を受けている人。
4．服用に際しては、説明書をよく読んでください。
5．J) 直射日光の当たらない湿気の少ない涼しい所に保管してください。
6．K) 小児の手の届かない所に保管してください。
7．L) 使用期限を過ぎた製品は服用しないでください。

Appendix

⑧ A) 鎮痛剤

販売名：ナロンエースＴ
（協力：大正製薬株式会社）

≪パッケージの記載≫
【効能】
 B) ☆頭痛・月経痛（生理痛）・歯痛・抜歯後の疼痛・腰痛・肩こり痛・筋肉痛・関節痛・打撲痛・ねんざにともなう痛み（ねんざ痛）・骨折痛・外傷痛・神経痛・咽喉痛（のどの痛み）・耳痛の鎮痛
☆悪寒（発熱によるさむけ）・発熱時の解熱

【用法・用量】
15 歳以上 C) 1回2錠、 D) 1日3回を限度とし、 C) なるべく空腹時を避けて G) 水又はぬるま湯で服用してください。
 E) 服用間隔は4時間以上おいてください。
 F) 15 歳未満は服用しないでください。

【注意】
1． H) 次の人は服用しないでください。
（1）本剤又は本剤の成分によりアレルギー症状を起こしたことがある人。
（2）本剤又は他の解熱鎮痛薬、かぜ薬を服用してぜんそくを起こしたことがある人。
（3）15 歳未満の小児。
（4）出産予定日 12 週以内の妊婦。
2． I) 服用後、乗物又は機械類の運転操作をしないでください。
3． J) 次の人は服用前に医師、歯科医師、薬剤師又は登録販売者に相談してください。
（1）医師又は歯科医師の治療を受けている人。
（2）妊婦又は妊娠していると思われる人。
（3）授乳中の人。
（4）高齢者。
（5）薬などによりアレルギー症状を起こしたことがある人。
（6）次の診断を受けた人。
心臓病、腎臓病、肝臓病、全身性エリテマトーデス、混合性結合組織病
（7）次の病気にかかったことがある人。
胃・十二指腸潰瘍、潰瘍性大腸炎、クローン病
4．服用に際しては、説明書をよく読んでください。
5． K) 直射日光の当たらない湿気の少ない涼しい所に保管してください。
6． L) 小児の手の届かない所に保管してください。
7． M) 使用期限を過ぎた製品は服用しないでください。

Appendix

⑨ A) 風邪薬

第②類医薬品
販売名：パブロンゴールドＡ〈微粒〉
（協力：大正製薬株式会社）

≪パッケージの記載≫

【効能】
　B) かぜの諸症状（せき、たん、のどの痛み、くしゃみ、鼻みず、鼻づまり、悪寒、発熱、頭痛、関節の痛み、筋肉の痛み）の緩和

【用法・用量】
次の量を食後なるべく 30 分以内に F) 水又はぬるま湯で服用してください。

年令	1回量	服用回数
C) 15 才以上	C) 1 包	1日3回
D) 12 才～14 才	D) 2/3 包	
E) 12 才未満　服用しないこと		

【注意】
1. G) 次の人は服用しないでください。
　　（1）本剤又は本剤の成分によりアレルギー症状を起こしたことがある人。
　　（2）本剤又は他のかぜ薬、解熱鎮痛薬を服用してぜんそくを起こしたことがある人。
2. H) 服用後、乗物又は機械類の運転操作をしないでください。
3. I) 授乳中の人は本剤を服用しないか、本剤を服用する場合は授乳を避けてください。
4. J) 次の人は服用前に医師、薬剤師又は登録販売者に相談してください。
　　（1）医師又は歯科医師の治療を受けている人。
　　（2）妊婦又は妊娠していると思われる人。
　　（3）高齢者。
　　（4）薬などによりアレルギー症状を起こしたことがある人。
　　（5）次の症状のある人。
　　　　高熱、排尿困難。
　　（6）次の診断を受けた人。
　　　　甲状腺機能障害、糖尿病、心臓病、高血圧、肝臓病、腎臓病、胃・十二指腸潰瘍、緑内障、呼吸機能障害、閉塞性睡眠時無呼吸症候群、肥満症
5. 服用に際しては、説明書をよく読んでください。
6. K) 直射日光の当たらない湿気の少ない涼しい所に保管してください。
7. L) 小児の手の届かない所に保管してください。
8. M) 使用期限を過ぎた製品は服用しないでください。

FOR FURTHER STUDY

Below is a useful list of sites for reference and further study.

厚生労働省：外国人向け多言語説明資料　一覧
  (Ministry of Health, Labour and Welfare: Multilingual Instruction Materials)
  https://www.mhlw.go.jp/stf/seisakunitsuite/bunya/0000056789.html

日本小児科学会：外国語での診療等に役立つ冊子・ウェブサイト
  (Japan Pediatric Society:Useful Materials for Medical Treatment)
  http://www.jpeds.or.jp/modules/activity/index.php?content_id=215

かながわ国際交流財団：多言語医療問診票
  (Kanagawa International Foundation: Multilingual Medical Questionnaire)
  http://www.kifjp.org/medical/

外国人医療センター MICA：多言語問診票
  (Foreign Medical Center: Multilingual Medical Questionnaire)
  https://npomica.jimdo.com/ 日本語 / 多言語 - 問診票 /

日本家庭薬協会：家庭薬の多言語商品情報
  (Home Medicine Association of Japan: Multilingual Product Information)
  http://www.hmaj.com/product.html

米国研究製薬工業協会：医療用医薬品の添付文書等の記載要領について英語版
  (The Pharmaceutical Research and Manufacturers of America: Instructions for Package Inserts of Prescription Drugs English Version)
  http://www.phrma-jp.org/library/phrma_efpia_translate20171225/

MSD Manual Consumer Version
  （MSD マニュアル家庭版）
  https://www.msdmanuals.com/en-jp/home

Mayo Clinic
  https://www.mayoclinic.org/

Medical News Today
  https://www.medicalnewstoday.com/

Very Well Health
  https://www.verywellhealth.com/

WebMD
  https://www.webmd.com/

著作権法上、無断複写・複製は禁じられています。

Medication Explained　Essential English for Pharmacists　　　[B-894]
現場で役立つ薬学英語表現

1　刷	2019 年 4 月 1 日

著　者	Glenn D. Gagné　　　　ガニエ・グレン
発行者 発行所	南雲　一範　　Kazunori Nagumo 株式会社　南雲堂 〒162-0801　東京都新宿区山吹町361 NAN'UN-DO Co., Ltd. 361 Yamabuki-cho, Shinjuku-ku, Tokyo 162-0801, Japan 振替口座：00160-0-46863 　TEL：03-3268-2311（営業部：学校関係） 　　　　03-3268-2384（営業部：書店関係） 　　　　03-3268-2387（編集部） FAX: 03-3269-2486
編集者	伊藤　宏実
組　版	H. I
装　丁	NONdesign
検　印	省略
コード	ISBN 978-4-523-17894-1　　C0082

Printed in Japan

E-mail　　nanundo@post.email.ne.jp
URL　　　http://www.nanun-do.co.jp/